REAL ESTATE

HOW TO SELL FOR MORE
AND BUY FOR LESS

ISBN 978-1-970071-02-3

Cover design and book design
©John H. Matthews, www.BookConnectors.com

Edited by Ginger Moran

Published by Bluebullseye Press

REAL ESTATE

HOW TO SELL FOR MORE
AND BUY FOR LESS

JUDY ARMSTRONG

CONTENTS

SECTION FOUR
CLIENT STORIES

SECTION FIVE
HOME LAYOUTS

SECTION SIX
THE NUTS AND BOLTS OF BUYING AND SELLING

Acknowledgements

A huge thank you to all those buyers and sellers I've met and sincerely tried to aid in their very important transactions over 36 years of practice as a real estate associate broker. Without them, this book could not have been written.

Under All is the Land

We are all affected by real estate in many ways! It is the only investment we can live and toast our toes by the fire in. Opening the door leads to comfort for both the body and the soul.

Let us not be overly sentimental lest we forget that for many people it is their major financial investment as well.

It stands to reason that all of us should be well informed about the subject of real estate and benefit from the experience of someone who has a wealth of knowledge garnered from 36 years in active real estate services and who holds professional degrees and several international awards.

Allow me to open the door and invite you in!

Many names have been changed to protect the innocent and the guilty.

Why Do You Need This Book?

Sprinkled through the following humorous stories which are all true, you'll find invaluable tips—whether you're buying, selling, or doing both at once. These tips could save you thousands of dollars.

Most of your preconceived notions about real estate are probably wrong, sad to say! Only by being in the trenches full time for many years can you expect to amass all this money-saving knowledge.

I'm happy to share my experiences and expertise with you, to make your buying and selling journey pleasant and successful.

Many names have been changed to protect the innocent and the guilty.

Preface

Always, in the back of my head, have been lines of poetry of William Wordsworth's I read so long ago: "The world is too much with us—Late and soon. Getting and spending we lay waste our powers."

This has haunted me and cropped up at the most inopportune times! Competing for 36 years in the very competitive world of real estate, I tried to shut it off but couldn't. After all, here I was with about 200 others in the same field, all vying for buyers and sellers, all without any benefits or salary. What a contradiction!

On my very first showing to a buyer, we were in a small ranch house in Verona. The nervous owner was seated on a couch near the basement door. As my clients started down the steps I heard a hissing sound and so turned around.

The owner said to me, "If you sell this, there's $500 extra bucks for you and you don't have to report it to your broker, either."

Of course, anything like this was a bribe and I had

no idea whether or not other people in the business would take such a thing.

In fact, I was totally unprepared for anything dishonest in this occupation—or in the world, I might add, having lived the sheltered life of a young lady. Then, like a deer in the headlights, I realized that there, on that top step to the basement, I had to decide how I would run my business—honestly or greedily.

I answered, "I don't do business that way." I've never looked back.

In this book you'll find amusing stories and informative ones. I have always found, through all the time I've been in the business, that behaving ethically and expecting the same of others has served me well.

SECTION ONE
LEARNING REAL ESTATE

CHAPTER ONE

Getting Started

Back in the 70's you had to know which firm you would be associated with before sitting for your licensure test, so I proudly wrote in the name of that firm. Just a few days later, the broker-owner called me and apologized but said that a realtor who had formerly been associated with his firm was coming back and they had no more room for me. I was beside myself! The exam was fast approaching, and I had to find another firm. I only knew two other brokers, so I called the first one who said he wasn't hiring at this time. So, holding my breath, I called the other one. He said "Well, come on down and let's talk about it." I was elated!

After I interviewed with Mr. Simmons he smiled and said in his soft drawl, "Well, I was really looking for a man to help me work the farms." My heart sank. "But," he went on, "I think we can add you to our realtors here."

I was happily at that firm for twelve years! He was a delightful broker with a wonderful sense of humor and an unbelievable store of knowledge about real estate transactions and how to make them work and about human nature. I learned so much about that from him!

One day I was wringing my hands over a seller who didn't want to look at the offer I had for him.

I said, "He said he doesn't really need to sell!"

Mr. Simmons answered, "When they say that, they usually do!"

I didn't know that! I was this innocent young girl who believed what people told me!

Another valuable lesson was "How Business Is Done in the South."

I saw an older gentleman come in—someone I knew who was an engineer with a big farm to sell. Mr. Simmons had invited him in as he had a proposition on the farm to discuss. It was never called an offer because that sounded weak and lower than the asking price.

The engineer entered Mr. Simmons' office. I can still picture him in his uniquely ugly black hard shoes with square-toed corners. He commented on a handsaw in the corner at which Mr. Simmons laughed and said, "That's my persuader. If I run into trouble with people about propositions, that's what I use!"

Uproarious laughter came out of his office.

I kept thinking. *Come on, Mr. Simmons, talk about the business!*

They must have made small talk and jokes for an hour! Finally, the proposition was discussed. By taking all that time to make small talk and jokes, Mr. Simmons had relaxed the client and put him in an agreeable mood. I recognized that as a brilliant strategy.

By the way, that's called "spittin' and whittlin'" in the South.

CHAPTER TWO

How It's Done: Education, Education, Education!

When I graduated from real estate school in the 70's I realized that it was the largest trade organization in the world for obvious reasons: you could get a license at age 18 if you studied and passed the test. In those days it was "Here's your desk and here's your phone. Pull up a chair—you're on your own."

I shared a desk with a part-timer and had one drawer (the right bottom) to call my own. I bought a notebook and brought in a telephone directory.

I began calling friends and neighbors to tell them that I was in business! I remember how difficult it seemed to learn such a myriad of facts about the business, including financing (math was always my bug-a-boo) and how startling it was to realize that there was no "one-size-fits-all" sales contract –that each one was entirely different. It would have been so easy just to learn one formula and change the names and dates.

Real estate was fun then, though! We had a one-page sales contract that was simple and direct—the names of the parties, the date, the legal description as well as the street address, the financing details and the date for settlement. As I later learned you had to remember to write in a termite inspection.

If the seller lived out of town I would simply place a long-distance call (which I recorded on a piece of paper, so my broker would know how much to charge me!) and read the offer. The seller would respond and, if it was accepted, I would ask him to send a telegram stating, "According to the offer my realtor read over the phone, I accept!" He would then accept the offer in writing with initials and signature when it arrived by mail two days later! We always said, "Your telegram will hold the offer."

Before long I realized that a lot of people wanted to choose a home before putting theirs on the market, so I had to ask my broker how to write up that kind of an offer and I can still spout off that complex paragraph today. The wording was extremely important and so, when I received an offer from another agent on one of my listings, often I would have to replace their wording with mine. Since no one likes to be corrected, this didn't endear me to other realtors, but I would stop at nothing to protect my seller.

Things began to click rather soon for me and my broker brought me a box with lined cards on it for me to record the names of my clients. That helped a lot! Shortly after that he offered me the unheated storage room in the back room of the office, so I could have my own desk and space to hang my coat. I was thrilled! Never mind that my chair was on top of the trap door to the basement! As a bonus I was allowed to decorate the room, so I busily painted the walls and hung some blue and green curtains with a cheerful floral pattern. Never mind that there was one small window up high and that the building next door blocked most of the light! It was mine!

Next my broker walked to the courthouse with me and showed me how to look up property in the gigantic, heavy deed books. That was so interesting! There were often plats that you could remove and copy, and clerks were there to help you. The room was full of lawyers— and me! Not many realtors took the time to do this. It was fascinating to follow a property deed's history back through time. Sometimes you could go through eight books to get the whole history.

I listened to records made by realtors about their methods to make more sales and I read lots of books and articles. I finally decided to apply for my first degree in the business called the G.R.I. (Graduate of Realtors' Institute). This degree allowed you to put those initials after your name, which was desirable to elevate you above those people in the trade organization who hadn't yet taken the time to further their education.

To obtain this degree, I commuted to Charlottesville for a week and took classes on different topics each day with instructors who were successful realtors. It was fun to be back in school again, and it was fantastic to ask questions of these instructors. I was floating on air after an instructor from California spoke about great sales techniques, but the next class was so solemn about the law and legal penalties that I was dashed on the rocks of despair.

After five days of classes we took tests in these topics and I was fortunate enough to pass and put my name and the GRI designation on all my business cards!

CHAPTER THREE

First Sales Lessons

We learned a lot to give us confidence when we were new at the game—tips like touting the firm's success record rather than our own and I found that to be a good ploy—and quite truthful. Gathering my courage, I drove to a nice suburban neighborhood of fairly new homes situated on one-acre lots with lovely mountain views. I had heard that one of the couples in that area was to be transferred with the trucking company where the husband worked, so I marched up to the front door. They politely invited me in with my sales charts and figures of my firm's success. Spreading them out, I complimented them on the style of their home which was quite avant garde for the time—an A-frame with wings and a cool loft room in the top of the letter "A." We toured, and I enjoyed seeing something new to me. Then we reviewed my papers and they said that it sounded fine and that they would list their home with me. I was overjoyed, watching them sign a listing of a whopping $85,000! That was a huge price in our county in 1978! I thanked them enthusiastically and promised to work hard to get it sold.

Looking back, it was a horrible listing because, before signing the contract, the sellers wrote down about eight names who were "exclusions"—in other words, if any of them bought it, I would receive no commission. In my heart I didn't think any of them would because they were all buying near a big factory quite far away from this neighborhood. (I was right, fortunately. It would be terrible to work hard and get paid nothing! Later I learned that this happened a lot in real estate.)

Forever etched in my memory is the sight of two young girls who were realtors giggling as they came up the front sidewalk, eager to apply for the listing on their house—the listing which I clutched in my hand!

I advertised the house as much as possible and put it out in the multiple listing service so that all the local realtors would be aware of it, and pretty soon a lovely lady realtor called with the exciting news that she had an offer from some policeman and his wife from New York who were retiring here. This realtor was as new as I was, and this was her very first offer. We were beside ourselves! She brought it to my office and we met in the large conference room (it was heated and had a big window) and we had the buyers with us as well. We bumbled through going over all the aspects of the offer, saying things like, "This is the way we usually do it!" In fact it was the first time either of us had done this. We gained confidence from each other and the buyers signed it.

About 10 days later the selling agent's husband called me. (He had also gotten his real estate license at the same time that we did). I could hear his wife crying in the background as he spoke. He explained that the buyers had gotten cold feet and made up a lot of excuses such as, they needed to store their furniture somewhere in the area before closing as their buyers in New York wanted them out and they drove back through their new neighborhood and saw a lot of trash in the gutters which was ugly. My sellers, who had moved, did not want to release them, of course, so we went to the attorney's office for settlement, but the buyers didn't show. It was so hard on all of us!

SECTION TWO
BUYERS AND SELLERS

CHAPTER FOUR

Helpful Hints for Both Buyers and Sellers

I cannot tell you how many military officers and CEO's—people used to being in charge—have been very problematic in the sale of their principal residences. They simply aren't used to allowing anyone else to take complete charge; therefore, the best tactic for a realtor is to schedule a long meeting with this seller, making suggestions and tossing them the ball so that they will feel that it's their idea!

It is wise to invite this seller's cooperation in making a list of printed information regarding the home's features to give the prospective buyers. Some sellers like to list improvements they have made to the property and include the dates for each.

They can also help with factual information about their location such as distance to schools, shopping, interstates, and other important places.

Other ideas for sellers who really want control might be:

- Create a diagram and names of all the plantings in the yard
- Write a personalized note about some of the things they have enjoyed about living here such as the sunsets from the patio
- Leave a list of repairmen who have installed roofing, appliances, etc.
- Have a kitchen drawer with the garage door opener, extra keys, warranties and instruction books for appliances.

The best advice is to leave for the showings!! You can explain that the buyer wants to see all the wonderful features of the home and whether the floor plan suits his needs. In order to do that, he will want to open all the closets and kitchen cabinets. He may even want to sit in a comfortable chair in the family room and just look out or around, which is a very good buying sign. If the seller is there, even in a different room, the buyer will feel intrusive, invasive, and downright rude doing any of this, and won't investigate. If he can't investigate, he is unlikely to buy. Most sellers understand this once you cheerfully explain that.

In other words, NEVER go in swinging and telling the seller that you're an expert in this field (even though you should be and probably are). It is likely to alienate the seller or at least make them stubborn.

Once I showed a house to a couple and the wife made very small little guttural noises like "Um hum" as she glided through the rooms. I later learned that the husband didn't want her to say anything because she had exclaimed enthusiastically about a house they bought the last time and he thought they paid too much because the sellers had been in earshot and knew how much she liked it.

I encouraged husbands who were looking at houses prior to the wife's trip to see them to make an offer subject to her approval in a certain time period because that was a legal contingency which would hold the house for them if the seller agreed to the price and terms. This worked like a charm 99% of the time and ended in a sale, but one time the transferring gentleman loved the house (and the garage, of course!) so he wrote an offer subject to his wife's approval. When I took her through it later she shook her head in the small, narrow kitchen and exclaimed, "I wonder why on this green earth he thought I would like this house!"

It just proves that there is truly an exception to every rule, even when you think you know each other after having lived together for years and years!

CHAPTER FIVE

CONNECTIONS & NETWORKING

The older I get the more I see the hand of my guardian angel in my life.

My parents packed up some of my grandmother's furniture after her funeral and put it on a moving van. I received a phone call from the truck driver at 8:00 Sunday morning saying that he was lost and asking directions. He finally arrived and started unloading. I was inconsolable because he had stacked heavy furniture on top of fragile little Victorian chairs with tufted velvet backs and delicate, curved legs, and several were broken as well as a pink marble coffee table top! All I could think of was how upset Nana would have been, so I was furious!

Someone suggested taking the furniture to a man in

town who could repair it. He was squirreled away above a real estate office in a little shop downtown. I took everything to him. Not only did he do a wonderful job, but he also introduced me to his son who was a good friend of a young man who was a realtor in Washington, DC. What a fortuitous connection that was!

The realtor was in the process of buying a large Staunton vacation home for relaxation during the summer months. Many of his Washington friends wished to do the same. Through him I was able to get many of my historic home listings sold. One of his Washington buddies bought three of my listings through the years. It was a great launch to my real estate career and never would have happened without the broken furniture!

I have always loved history, so I feel very blessed to be able to practice real estate in an area so rich in historic homes and buildings. As a result, I was thrilled when a gentleman, a retired general and friend, called me to list his family homestead where he and his wife, daughter, and two sons had lived for 40 years. I couldn't wait to research it!

I went to City Hall to look it up and started tracing it. My search eventually led me to the Court House basement where old, dusty field drawers lay sleeping, most undisturbed. I pulled one out and saw a purple ribbon surrounding lots of papers. Pay dirt! There was stationary with lovely pictures at the top of corseted females in long dresses carrying parasols staring down from an upstairs balcony that was no longer there! This beautiful three-story traditional home was once Sherwood Female Academy, which explained lots of things! There were letters from the Headmaster imploring the grocer not to expect quick payment of the bill with such beautifully expressed tender sentiment. I couldn't wait to share them with the General, who had never known of their existence.

From this beginning, I learned a lot more history. In order to raise more money to pay the bills, the school sold off lots of its land and the lots became today's Sherwood Avenue. Original homes built on it dated from 1880 to 1900. The competition between girls' schools was very intense as there were about six of them at that time.

Within that house, history literally spoke to me as I saw the name "Josie Bush, 1888" etched in the window glass on the third floor, which served as a dormitory. On the white plaster wall in one room up there you could see a list of dresses and what time of day you would attire yourself in each!

The General had an original Jed Hotchkiss map (he was Lee's cartographer) that was hanging on the stairway wall. He said it should stay with the house!

The General was very parsimonious and said that the new buyer needed to know that he wanted to save two of the boxwoods in the rose garden for his and his wife's graves. Oh, and the dining room draperies that were floor to ceiling (and the ceilings were high) should be saved to go in their new compact town house. His wife talked him out of that one!

He was very much a gentleman of the old school so suggested that these "guests" who toured his home might enjoy a glass of sherry in the library after their tour! Of course, he had no concept that today's clients usually have a very busy schedule and might have eight house showings in one day so they're here for a limited time.

He had difficulty speaking after a stroke and so wanted to be a gracious host. One heartless female realtor told me that she and her client had no time to stand there and be patient with him, so she directed me to keep him busy while they went through the house!

CHAPTER SIX

SIGNS SELL!

I once knew a gentleman with a very impressive Southern Colonial home on over an acre in town. It was majestic and certainly one of the most beautiful houses in town. One day he called and told me that he wanted me to list it, but he didn't want a sign. He told me that he didn't think a sign would sell his home, but that his home needed an expensive advertising campaign targeting people in the Northern Virginia area.

I protested politely and told him that I had a beautiful sign which hung from a wooden post and was in very good taste. Finally, he relented.

Two days later, a man drove by it and called me saying, "I've always loved that house! I want to see it right away!"

Instead of a buyer from Northern Virginia or further away that the seller thought I'd need to attract with an expensive advertising campaign, here came a buyer in two days who lived four blocks away!

One evening at a party, I ran into a friend who said, "Judy, we desperately want to live on one of those streets near the college, but we drive up there all the time and there's nothing for sale!"

I answered right away, "Oh, but there is! The seller just doesn't want a sign." The seller's wife was in a nursing home 100 miles away. The seller drove to see her all the time, but he was very particular about who the buyer would be and had a real fear of signs and people overwhelming him to see his house. I called the listing realtor on the spot to see when we could view the property. My friend and her husband wrote an offer right away.

One day in a sales meeting, my broker said, "You know, people tend to forget a property is still for sale if it was on the market a while ago and the signs have fallen down or gotten lost. So I think we should put them back on those unsold, rather undesirable lots— the ones that go straight downhill from the street in that lovely subdivision in town."

Not two days later, the office phone rang. A gentleman who was enjoying breakfast in his stately Southern Colonial home gazed out the window at the lovely woods across the street and saw—oh no!—a real estate sign!

His first thought was, "Oh no! My lovely view would be ruined if a house goes up there! My deer! My beautiful autumn leaves!"

He was definitely interested in purchasing that piece of wooded property! He did so and put a driveway through those trees and built a storage building down at the bottom of the hilly lot. Later he was able to acquire additional forest land adjoining the first lot for his son, who then built a lovely home there.

The remaining lots were snapped up when building lots became scarce, as always happens. But without the signs, they may either never have sold or taken much longer to be noticed and to sell.

One day a gentleman who was staying at a lovely bed and breakfast on Staunton's stately East Beverley Street decided to take a morning stroll.

He was so appreciative of the large homes and the great variety exhibited in their architecture. In the front yard of the fourth house he was admiring, there was a lady bending over her flowers, gardening in her pearls and white gloves.

He cleared his throat and said, "Excuse me, madam, but I am in awe of the majestic homes on this street. I do wish one were for sale—I would buy it!"

She paused and returned his gaze.

"Well," she said quietly, "that one is." She pointed to the house next door to where they were standing. She then added, "The owner didn't want a sign. She thinks they're tacky."

The gentleman made a slight bow, thanked her, and marched up the sidewalk next door.

Long story short, he bought it and has lived there happily ever since!

SECTION THREE
CHOOSING YOUR PROFESSIONALS

CHAPTER SEVEN

YOUR REALTOR AND HER SUPPORT STAFF

What are the duties of an airline pilot? Does he make your reservation, print your boarding pass, load your luggage onto the plane, serve snacks and drinks, etc.? Or does he simply fly the plane?

He does his job, which is to fly the plane; all of the less urgent duties are delegated to someone else.

Yet this is not what people expect of a realtor and sometimes we fall into this trap and end up writing ads at midnight because there simply was no time during the action-packed day.

When computers came on the scene it became obvious that we couldn't spend our time out pressing the flesh and looking for leads in the computer at the same time and carry them both off really well.

There are many auxiliary positions that can be filled by the right person that will free up the realtor to mix and mingle, join organizations, and list and sell property.

It would be an over simplification if I left it at that. You can hire people to fill slots such as buyer specialist, transaction specialist, runner, and executive assistant, but unless they are family members who know how you work and what you expect, it's difficult to get people who share your vision and your work ethic! I had three or four executive assistants before I got the right one as well as several Buyer Specialists.

As a realtor, you must spend your time on activities that result in earning money since there is no salary. Writing ads and putting signs in the ground do not earn you money. I realized that this sort of thing must be delegated—particularly putting signs in, taking them out, hanging key safes on doors, and all that—so I hired a gal who knew the county quite well to take ads to the paper and all the tasks that required running around.

My executive assistant saved me from burial alive! I had tried several who were not satisfactory, but the third was the charm and we stayed together for about 18 years! She had been executive secretary to nine vice presidents at once in a corporate setting, so she was more than qualified for the job I needed her to perform! She was so good that she had a tray on the desk with paper work for long-range projects and she would reach into that when all the immediate tasks were completed.

She freed me up to get new business while she politely called our sellers to give them feedback on showings of their property. Sometimes she had to call the realtor who showed our listing repeatedly to get what his buyer's comments were, too!

My sellers enjoyed her calls; she was so personable on the phone. She reminded me of all kinds of things like deadlines and was absolutely invaluable!

Real estate around here peaked in value—the demand became greater than the supply—in 2005 and 2006, which changed the playing field as well as the rules! Competition for property became fierce. Some realtors didn't adjust to the change and kept writing the same verbiage in their contracts, which did not serve their buyers well!

Now it was necessary to use an acceleration clause— clean from the big cities in Northern Virginia—which addressed the fact that there might be competing offers submitted at the same time and, if so, how high the bidder was willing to go and in what increments, or whether or not he would eliminate a home inspection. It was wild for our little town.

One day my assistant hit upon a very useful discovery and I don't know that anyone else did! She said, "I've found that if I go into the Multiple Listing Site about 4:00 I can see what's getting ready to come out tomorrow!"

Wow! This was fantastic news!

For example, I had three clients looking for historic homes in the downtown area—scarce as the proverbial hens' teeth—and my assistant found several this way on different days. I raced to the phone and called my buyer clients and advised them to drop everything and go with me that evening and write an offer immediately if they liked it because the next day everyone would know about it and they would be in competition and could lose it. My clients were eternally grateful to me for this service and I was so grateful to my assistant!

Now it should be dawning on the realtor that part time realtors are doing a terrible disservice to their clients. This has never been and will never be "something to do in my spare time." Realtors are supposed to be agents for their clients, which they can't possibly be if they're not on top of the market as well as being well informed about the industry with its constant changes.

CHAPTER EIGHT

HOW DID YOU CHOOSE YOUR DOCTOR?

Was it because he or she sits next to you in church or is your son's Cub Scout Leader? I ask because these are some of the answers I get when I ask how a person chose their realtor to sell their house. It illustrates clearly that we're comfortable choosing someone "like me." Realtors have fought this concept for many years with ads about their professional designations and their meaning. It seems to fall on deaf ears for the most part, but I submit that for many people their home represents their largest, most important investment, and to entrust its care to just anyone with a real estate license can be one of your most costly mistakes!

So, what's important to look for when you make your selection? When I needed laparoscopic surgery for a painful gall stone I went to a surgeon whom I knew personally as well as by reputation and I asked him point blank how many of these surgeries he had performed and if they were all successful. He answered, "That's fair." And he had done many hundreds.

Experience is very important when you choose an agent to represent you in real estate, but it's not the only factor by any means. You should see what professional designations the realtor holds for several reasons.

1. This person has invested considerable time and money to acquire this knowledge - knowledge that can protect you in this very important transaction.

2. This person can see red flags while they're still yellow and head off possible problems and he or she can make sure that the wording in your listing and sales contracts is understood by you and are protective of your best interests.

3. You should also look for leadership roles in organizations the realtor belongs too, which show an interest in his or her community.

As in the practice of law, realtors' interests and fields of expertise vary widely. I know men for example, who hate to show land and get "their trouser cuffs dirty," and I wouldn't want to list my county acreage with them. Conversely, I know a man who was a very successful realtor who loved only land and called me if it had a house on it to list the house.

There are realtors who specialize in historic homes and those who really prefer brand new ones. And of course, the commercial realtor is another breed of cat!

As a Referral Realtor I can access this information all around the world quite easily and it's free to my clients.

Talking to client

writing ads
for listings

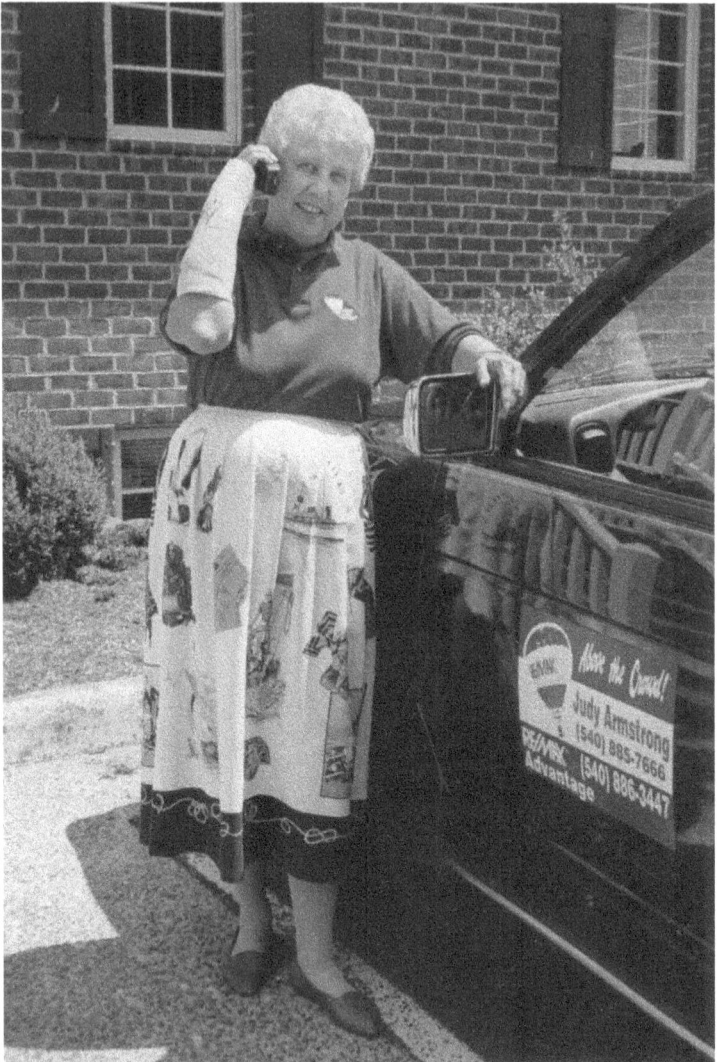

SECTION FOUR
CLIENT STORIES

CHAPTER NINE

THE CLIENT WITH THE SANDY MUSTACHE

This tall, distinguished gentleman arrived here from the DC area with his equally tall, stately young wife, and captured the town with their charm. He was a lover of the theatre and was in many local productions and rumor had it that he had once appeared in an opera, carrying a spear! I remember him intoning, "The play's the thing" and he gave the phrase new meaning. He was standing in front of my fireplace in his blue blazer with the brass buttons, twirling his mustache.

He said, "You can go any place in a blue blazer!" And he did.

The beautiful home they bought for their personal residence had belonged to a General, which pleased my client immediately—or, rather, it started his thought process until he exclaimed, "I think I'll call myself,

'Captain.' I like the sound of that: 'Captain' Jones."

Their home could be entered from two different streets and they often liked to stroll down the pleasant street to the rear with its sidewalks, shade trees, and pretty Victorian homes. He had rehearsed a polite dialogue, he told me, because many older ladies lived there and were enchanted by the sight of this big, burly man pushing a baby carriage and he found it hard to break away politely. What he said was this, "Oh, I have so enjoyed talking to you, but Diana and I have a roast in the oven and it's almost time to take it out. Good bye for now!"

Diana's parents had warned her before she married him saying he would never amount to anything, but she didn't care because she loved him. Her parents were quite right, but the couple seemed very happy anyway.

One day he had a wild hare and called out of the blue saying, "Judy, we know it's crazy but we just want to look at this house—that's all—we just want to go inside."

The home was magnificent and had a long history involving some very well-known patriots including Thomas Jefferson. It was owned by a lady who had moved away and it had recently come on the market. We climbed a great number of steps and pulled open the heavy door. I gasped! We were facing an entrance hall that I exclaimed must be 40 feet wide and 12 feet to the wall facing us. (I later measured—it was 39 feet). He and his wife bought it with the idea of turning it into an elegant club.

I couldn't wait to show an historic hotel property to these prospective buyers! Once a commanding brick building on an important corner in town, it was now scarred and tattered from years of neglect and homeless tenants, but there were tax credits and the glory available to its savior from many citizens of our town. Breathlessly, I opened the front door and entered a worn-out bus depot occupying what had once been an impressive hotel lobby. Undeterred, I marched through and opened the first door I saw. In the darkness I could barely make out the outline of many steps descending— but wait! What was that gurgling noise? I reached for the dangling light bulb and switched it on. Wonder of wonders – Lewis Creek was bubbling merrily through the basement!

I turned helplessly to my client who was twirling his sandy mustache and, without skipping a beat, commented, "Well, there are two things you could do: You could offer boat rides, or you could keep the door shut."

I cracked up! Did I ever love showing property to this man and his wife and getting free entertainment. As fate would have it, they actually bought four beautiful, historic homes from me, but not that building!

I once had the pleasure of getting to know an elderly gentleman who had grown up in the Staunton area and told me interesting stories of the old days. One of these was regarding Lindbergh's visit. His father had gotten him out of school, so he could meet the great man when he flew his famous plane to a long, grassy spot near Deerfield and landed. He was the guest of a prominent Staunton citizen who had a summer retreat there and Lindbergh would be able to relax, hunt and fish.

The elderly gentleman told me that he had served in the CIA and had had a most interesting career but had come back home to retire and buy a home for his sister and her husband who had fallen on hard times—in fact, they had to soon be out of their home. He had cash to buy a nice place for them and was happy that he could do so.

He did specify that he wanted one particular lawyer—a woman—and no one else. So he wrote a contract and when it was accepted I delivered it to his lawyer. We looked forward to a quick closing.

The home he had selected was a nice brick ranch west of town with a mountain view, some acreage that featured a tennis court near the road and attractive landscaping.

It all seemed so simple! That's when you have to watch out, I guess! He had chosen this lawyer for a good reason: She was very thorough. She worked way ahead of closing and was just one of those well-organized people.

Several weeks before the big day she let us know there was a title problem—a big one! It seemed that the Highway Department had never officially closed off the old state highway that once ran through this property (right through the tennis courts!) so theoretically they could reopen it at any time. Now, we know that as a practical matter this "ain't happenin'"; however, it was a huge blemish on the title and every buyer wants a clear title and its assurance (an insurance!)

She told us that she would submit everything to VDOT (The Highway powers that be) in Richmond and that when they put it on the docket they would most likely clear it.

So, I wondered, how soon would this take place? It turned out not to be a matter of great urgency to them so we waited all summer long before those poor folks could move in!

"It Ain't Closed 'Til It's Closed!"

P.S. I must reveal that this home had been sold twice in the previous ten years. One of the buyers had been my client. In both sales, the purchaser's male lawyer had missed this fact in the title search they did.

CHAPTER TEN

ANIMAL STORIES

Animal Story # 1

The little boy Charles was adorable with big blue eyes and eyelashes that any girl would envy—long, dark, and curled up at the ends—and he was a very observant and quick learner. He communicated easily with his deaf parents using signs and smiles or frowns, and with the rest of the world with his ever-expanding English vocabulary.

When I went to pick them all up, he was crouching down in that doubled up squat known only to the very young and Chinese of all ages who talk and smoke an entire cigarette in that cramped position!

In front of him and stretching clear across the tiled kitchen floor was a long trail of dog treats, at the other end of which a puppy was happily munching his way towards us.

Leaving the busy pup behind we piled into my car to look at houses.

In the living room at the first home an elderly lady was reclining on the sofa stroking a cat. She told us not to pet him as he was sick. Charles regarded him soberly and then followed us around the house as we entered each room, pulled open the closet doors, and generally looked around.

Next, we drove to a small house where the owners greeted us and said that they had a cat in their home, but that he was hiding under the bed as he was very shy. She lifted up the dust ruffle, so we could see the cat. Charles went into his squat and reached out his little hand, causing the cat to retreat farther under the bed.

We were soon driving to the third house since the people hadn't found the home yet that would be right for them. This time no one greeted us, and I had to use my key to unlock the front door. It was a newly constructed home and still smelled like freshly cut wood.

By now Charles knew the drill and rushed on ahead of us. We found him in the last bedroom staring inside the closet. His mother asked him in sign language what he was doing.

He signed back to her, "Looking for the cat!"

As with hearing children who are too young to pronounce each word clearly and correctly, children sometimes don't make the exact sign for the word. He was smearing the fingers of one hand in a downward motion across his cheek. I asked his mother, in my feeble sign language, what his sign meant, and she showed me the correct sign for a cat's whiskers, saying he was too young to do it right, but, as in the hearing world, she understood what he was trying to express.

Learning ASL (American Sign Language) opened new doors for me when I realized that I could perform a valuable and much needed service for the deaf by explaining the home buying process to them and realizing that many deaf people were renting when they could actually purchase!

Animal Story # 2

A young couple called me to say that they were moving to Roanoke, so I went to their house perched on a high hill above the street. They had a two-year old son and a large female Labrador retriever named Sue. The dog had become extremely protective of the little boy and thus hated intruders.

The parents said, "Just say, 'Sue, go to your chair!' whenever clients come in."

There was a living room chair next to a window where Sue enjoyed sitting and gazing out at the construction taking place across the street. I happened to have the first showing and Sue came to the door snarling and growling so I gave her the command and she left the back door, turning her head and growling all the way to her chair. I had to put this under "showing instructions" in the listing for all the realtors to read!

Animal Story # 3

Some friends of mine were selling a charming vintage house on a well-loved street that had a rather unusual strange situation: in the den which had a very high ceiling, there were attic openings on each side, and there were resident bats in the attic. The owners were used to having them appear sometimes as they were reading in the den, flying high above their heads.

The owners decided to move to the country, so they engaged a realtor, and, on such a popular street, they were under contract before long.

The home inspection was very hard on this old home, so the sellers were upset and indignant and felt that the report was trying to make an old house new, which sometimes happens.

The sellers began making repairs and updates and were working towards closing when suddenly they looked at each other and smiled. They said in unison, "Let's not tell them about the bats."

It gave them comfort to picture the scene when the bats would first fly over the buyers' heads!

Animal Story # 4

I represented the seller when a friend bought a nice old country house and moved in. He and his wife had a great sense of humor and were old buddies of mine. They worked hard to create a beautifully landscaped yard in back with water cascading off stones and lovely blooming plants.

One night they invited me over for dinner, so I went and toured the house and then we sat in back by the pretty waterfall.

Suddenly an animal parade marched single file by our chairs! Two dogs, a cat, and a chicken. I love dogs, so I patted the heads of each one in turn and then the chicken strutted by, bringing up the rear.

I thought, "Well, what am I to do? I guess I'll pat it on the head, too," which I did. Immediately it fluttered and became airborne and landed on my head!

I had no preparation for this sort of activity and just then I felt a warm sticky liquid begin to drop through my hair and down my face.

The hostess, wringing her hands, ran to the kitchen and returned hurriedly with a roll of paper towels! After shooing the chicken off my head and rubbing my hair I dashed into the kitchen and stuck my head under the kitchen faucet! It was truly an unforgettable evening!

German Dogs

I don't trust any dogs that are German because I have had frightening experiences with almost all German breeds.

The first was when I was waving to a neighbor from my car. I rolled down the window to shout a greeting as he was on the front porch of his hill top house. He had a Doberman named, appropriately, "Rommel" and suddenly Rommel ran head long down the front yard hill and charged into my car furiously barking and showing dagger-like white teeth in my window! Scary!

Another incident involving a German dog took place in Highland County in a lovely mountainside cabin. I had bid the owners goodbye after a visit with them and their two little dachshunds. I had petted them, and they seemed fine with company. Forgetting my gloves, I went to the back door and opened it and the dogs jumped straight up and wrapped their teeth around my wrists!

The last event involving a German breed is the worst. I was showing a beautiful Southern Colonial home in the countryside around Staunton that had a Rottweiler in residence. Walking through the farm yard behind I saw evidence of his terrible personality—a goat he had torn limb from limb!

The most unusual pet story I encountered involved a small ranch home north of Staunton in which the owner confined his hobby to glass cages encircling the basement walls. Each cage housed a snake. Several of us wouldn't enter this home when it was on a real estate tour.

CHAPTER ELEVEN

SELLERS SAY THE DARNDEST THINGS!

Sellers Know the House;
They Don't Know the Prospective Buyers
An older couple put their house on the market and really thought they could help sell the place if they were present for the showings. After all, they knew the house better than anyone! The nice young realtor took the prospective buyers into the den and they all stood looking at the large fireplace. The owners extolled its virtues saying that it gave off so much heat and had such wonderful high blazes.

The realtor and the clients of his walked speedily through the bedrooms and beat a hasty retreat after that. The clients were house hunting after a fire had burnt their house to the ground!

In another instance the realtor, noting that the sellers were home, rang the bell and the sellers admitted them into their beloved home.

"Oh," they said, "we've just loved this house and reared our four daughters here, but now they're gone and it's just the two of us so it's way too big."

And who are the people looking at the house? People whose children had married and left. They thought the house suitable for their retirement, entertaining, and hobbies, but, after they talked to the owners, they thought it might be too big!

A crusty old Colonel and his wife decided to sell and move near one of their children. They had loved their home and were continually having parties and dinners for Army friends and were so busy with this that it looked like it would be a huge task to get them to leave for showings! In addition, the Colonel was accustomed to being in charge and didn't want to release any control to the realtor. I really had my work cut out for me on this one!

He insisted in leading me into every nook and cranny of the house and lecturing on what they were going to do in various rooms but hadn't done (which is a complete waste of time) and he particularly wanted me to see the type of window locks he had installed on each window. He wanted every prospective buyer to see this feature!

For the first few showings he would tag along and point out this feature. I simply could not get through to him that if the floor plan didn't suit, the locks on the windows wouldn't magically convince people to buy it. I convinced him that I would print out folders about the house and include the window lock information in the folder and I also eventually was successful in getting the owners to leave for the showings. Of course, that was when it sold.

As time went on some owners actually prepared slide shows of their landscaping in all 4 seasons which would change automatically, and I thought this was a great thing! A picture, in this case, was truly worth 1,000 words!

Staging houses to sell can be very useful as many homes can be more appealing to a broader buyer base with expert advice: "You live in your house one way; you sell it in another."

Examples of what not to do include (but are not limited to): having collections of objects which can look like clutter to a buyer, having furniture too large for the room, having too much furniture in the room, having closets crammed with clothes (some should be removed to another place or, if none is available, hung on pipes in the basement.)

Some owners are quite savvy about preparing their home to show well. I remember one of my sellers had a showing on a snowy February morning, so he prepared a roaring fire and had soft music playing. There was also an aroma of baking wafting through the house. The prospective buyers fell over themselves getting back to the office to write an offer. I told my sellers that if they sprayed the oven door with one of those cooking scents they could turn the heat on low and it would smell as if they were baking something.

Another valuable trick for sellers is my 10 minutes showing notice rule:

NEVER turn potential buyers away because they might be your buyers and they will probably never come back. If the realtor is there at your door apologizing because they're early or late or had no appointment but were driving by and really want to see your house, this is your script:

"Please walk around the yard and look in the garage, tool shed, patio, whatever – and come back to this door in a few minutes."

Now you stuff the toys, newspapers, whatever is all over into a pre-ordained spot (dishwasher? car? under or behind sofa?) and smile sweetly at the door.

CHAPTER TWELVE

DEAL KILLERS

Selling the house can become really stressful as well as unsuccessful under certain conditions, and I've encountered all of these:

A renter who, if present for the showings, recites a tale of woe about living there such as very high utility bills, cold drafts, neighbors who are obnoxious, and the like.

A rebellious teenager who doesn't want to move to another school district and consequently trashes her room before showings.

A barking yelping dog in a cage in the house who yelps the whole time the house is shown.

People who leave their house in a terrible mess with unswept floors, unmade beds and piles of dirty laundry in many rooms. (It's pretty bad when the potential buyers turn to me and ask, "Do they know the house is on the market?")

Home Inspectors. These people come with a variety of backgrounds and until recently in Virginia were merely certified rather than licensed. In my past dealings with them, I submitted a "partial list of some home inspectors my clients have used" so that my client could interview them and pick one they wanted. Some were previously contractors but they all had different backgrounds. Some were deal killers who seemed to delight in frightening buyers. Some were so inaccurate that they said the furnace didn't work (forcing the seller to drive 100 miles to the house in order to flick the right switch on), or they said that the septic system needed repairs when the property was served by sewer.

Realtors do NOT recommend. Realtors are there to furnish unbiased information, so the client can make choices. Further the seller sometimes offers a home inspection he has recently had performed to the Buyer if he wants to accept that and save the cost. That is the buyer's decision!

I once saw a home inspector claim that the seller I represented needed an expensive update to her electrical system. I then suggested that we call in an electrician with many years of experience to install what was needed. He explained that we didn't need an expensive update since there was something in the present system that made it unnecessary. I drew the conclusion after several years in the real estate business that if I were buying a house, I would call in experienced electricians, plumbers, contractors, etc., rather than a home inspector.

CHAPTER THIRTEEN

SUCCESS STORIES

Mr. & Mrs. Bond. James Bond.

Here's a true story that's hard to believe! One morning I got a phone call from somewhere in England and was pleased to hear that lovely British accent on the other end.

This man declared enthusiastically: "We've just viewed our dream house on your web site!"

I could hardly wait to continue this conversation!

"Yes," he went on, "It's the lovely large white one with dark green shutters! It's perched on lush acreage above the road. It has an inviting patio in back and it's only two years old!"

"Well," I answered, "are you moving to the states?"

"Yes," he said, "my wife is from the Charlottesville

area which wouldn't be far and that is exactly the type of home we want."

"Great," I continued, "but you're in England. How soon can you see it?"

He said, "I can be there in two days. I've been to Staunton before and I know where the train station is. I could meet you there."

Then he added, "I will carry a copy of The London Times under my arm. That should make identification certain."

"Oh," I mused, "how marvelously British!"

It all seemed like a dream and I wondered if this would actually happen! With racing heart (and a key to the white house), I drove to the station at the appointed hour. I beheld a tall, stately gentleman in a business suit carrying a furled umbrella (of course!) with the London Times under his other arm! Oh, sheer delight! We talked a lot about London (I had been there several times) and drove along the scenic road to this property about five miles west of town.

He was very happy to see it in person and carefully explored each room, explaining that since his wife couldn't come, he would have to phone her and describe the details. Back to my office we went and made a long, long, long distance call. I tried not to think of dollar signs with wings on them! Her reaction was very favorable, so she told him to go ahead and buy it! I'll never forget that thrill!

A Memorable Shower

Some old and dear friends listed their beautiful two-story traditional brick home with me and I was delighted to go to work for such great people.

One day the lady of the house was upstairs in the shower when she heard the loudest crash imaginable and thought, "WHAT WAS THAT??"

What had happened really needs to be shown in slow motion movie—words cannot describe it—and the movie makers in Hollywood would have rejected this script as just too impossible! I will nevertheless attempt to describe it in my poor words.

Directly across the street from my client's two-story colonial was a single-story ranch-style house situated on a corner lot. The two driveways were directly across from each other.

In the single-story ranch-style house across the street lived a local car dealer, his wife, and their young son. Said young son came home and left his car in the driveway without putting the emergency brake on. Said car slowly began to roll backwards. It crossed the hump in the middle of the street and headed straight for my client's two-car garage, which had a brick post in the center, separating the two parking spaces. The neighbor's car went in the opening on the unoccupied right side of the garage perfectly, not even grazing the center post, and crashed through the fireplace into the living room which was under the master suite, and of course, the shower!

As a P.S., we had to stop all showings until a new garage wall and a new fireplace were built! The man of the house told me that the new construction was the strongest fireplace wall in the State of Virginia!

A Library of One's Own

I once had the assignment of finding a home for the incoming officer of a college and his wife, a music professor. They had a collection of 2,000 books that had to be housed and they only liked newer homes—oh, and it had to be about five minutes from the college. This was such a tall order because the homes near the college were historic and dated from about 1850 to 1920. They were architecturally amazing and highly desirable for most people but not for them! There was only one newer neighborhood that might work, but nothing there was for sale. They absolutely had to identify a home before leaving town to go back to their present college jobs so we earmarked one that was a little too far and a little too small. They left town putting on a brave smile.

Two days later the perfect home came on the market in that neighborhood where nothing had been for sale! I called and said, "Your house just came on the market! Can you come?"

They responded that they would love to, but they couldn't leave the college where they worked again so soon! They said, "Take pictures! Send them!"

I wasted no time. I took pictures of the surroundings as well as every room in the house including bathrooms and laundry. They were overjoyed and decided they could have bookshelves built in the walk-out basement and did I know someone who could build them?

Yes, I did!

They said, "Mail the contract!"

 I did!

They wanted a home inspection so, when we coordinated that with their arrival date here (with their furniture in a truck!), I told them I'd meet them at the house with the inspector.

So there they were, on the doorstep waiting to see their home for the first time!

I held my breath as we paraded through it and they said things like, "Oh, this must be a linen closet. Oh, these steps must go to an outside basement entrance."

Fortunately, they really liked it! Phew! What a responsibility!

CHAPTER FOURTEEN

IT'S AN ILL WIND THAT BLOWS NO GOOD IN REAL ESTATE!

As my first broker, Mr. Simmons, once intoned, "It's an ill wind that blows no good in real estate!"

I found this to be true when Staunton had a rare event occur the night before Easter Sunday—an ice storm. All the trees had long, icy fingers and the streets were skating rinks. Announcements were made about church services being cancelled—on Easter Sunday! Families had swollen in size as college-aged children who were concerned about their aging parents had come home for Easter.

Some parents lived in venerable old mansions with many steps and rooms that they rarely visited, so these visiting sons and daughters decided it was time for them to move!

I was very busy helping families transition from large, historic homes into townhouses at this time!

Making Marriages in My Dishpan

I have found that when I do dishes, it frees up my mind to wander and do some serious problem-solving. On this particular day, I'd had some old friends come to me with a specific buying request but with a strict budget. At first glance, it seemed like an insolvable problem.

They had beautiful antiques and knew that the heat system must be radiator hot water because hot air would dry them out. They needed several fairly large rooms to display their Oriental rugs. But the real kicker was that they needed to be not too far from horseback riding, which was their passion!

At first blush this was an impossible combination because when horses entered the picture, we most certainly would be in the county on some acreage, and land would drive the price even higher. I had shown them several possibilities, hoping to increase their budgetary restraints, but to no avail.

I started dwelling on the problem as I did dishes. Suddenly, a house with an adequately sized living and dining room and radiators with hot water heat floated into my mind. I knew it well since it was my listing. Alas! It was about $5,000 too high. I stewed over that and also remembered how firm the owners were on their price.

I decided to visit these homeowners and talk about the listing again. I remarked that they had included a washer, dryer, and other appliances and wondered aloud if they could keep them and offer their home for $5,000 less? (The reason I really wanted this to work was that the home was in walking distance of a horse farm!)

The owners agreed to this new plan and both buyers and sellers were absolutely delighted!

My happiness was complete when my old real estate course teacher, who saw the sale go through, congratulated me with a phone call!

"Nice sale," he said.

Baldwin Acres Mix-Up

A realtor who wasn't very familiar with the Baldwin Acres neighborhood set off with his client to go through a house she wanted to see there. He was anxiously looking for it when he spotted the name of the seller on a mailbox, so he pulled in the driveway. There was no real estate sign, but some people didn't want them, so he didn't think much of that.

Reaching the back door, he tried the handle and it opened. He thought that the seller had left for the showing and left the back door unlocked. They went all through the home and went out the back door. Just then the lady of the house pulled up, looking very startled. The Realtor said, "We all just love your house! Thank you for leaving the back open."

The surprised lady responded, "It's not on the market! I just ran to the grocery because I'm baking a cake and was out of vanilla!" Then she added, "There is a house on the market two blocks away and the seller's name is the same as ours. Let me give you their address."

That lady couldn't wait to tell her friends about that one!

CHAPTER FIFTEEN

TRIO: 3 BANKERS

Banker #1

One of my neighbors, a well-liked banker, had his house up for sale due to his being transferred. His buyer only lived a few blocks away and was a friend, which made it a stress-free and very pleasant transaction. The buyer and the seller each had a realtor, but instead of the usual formalities the banker-seller offered his friendly buyer a key so he could come and measure for curtains at his convenience before settlement. They also discussed among themselves the TV antenna on the roof and whether the buyer might like to purchase it. He said he had to think about it.

One evening as dusk settled on the rooftop and its antenna, the buyer decided to walk over to the house and measure for the curtains, so he entered and climbed the stairs to the bedrooms. As he stretched the measuring tape over a front window he heard a car pull up on the street, stop, and he saw the banker-seller emerge and raise the trunk. What he saw next he could hardly believe! His friend started to rock the mailbox stand back and forth, working harder and harder, until at last it came out of the ground. He shoved the whole thing into his trunk and tied down the lid and then drove off.

At settlement soon after the seller asked his friend if he wanted to buy the TV antenna. The buyer smiled and said, "I'm still thinking about it."

Banker #2

I had a neighbor who was a very popular banker with many friends. He lived in an attractive Cape Cod home near me. I had just begun my real estate career and was delighted that he asked me to look for a house that matched his criteria. It was pretty simple, really, because he wanted a house with some charm, south of town in the county. To emphasize and further clarify he said in his serious banker voice, "Not a ranch style and not as far south as Mint Spring."

I searched the listings diligently each day, hoping that something appealing would pop up in his price range. About ten days later I saw a listing come on the market that I thought would really merit his attention!

I called him instantly and he said, "Oh, I've been meaning to tell you. We bought a house."

My heart dropped in my shoes! Recovering myself I feigned enthusiasm and said, "Oh, great! What and where is the house?"

He said, "It's a brick ranch in Mint Spring." He added, "We saw a notice about an auction there Saturday, so we decided to go, and it was a good deal."

At this point many realtors would throw up their hands and shout, "All buyers are liars!"

They would be missing an important lesson. What most bankers want to buy is not a house but a "deal." Their motivation is strictly financial! A good realtor always digs deeper and tries to look at the hunt through the eyes of the buyer.

About five years later this gentleman called me and wanted me to list his brick ranch because he was heading to a new banking job in Florida. To prepare the home for the market he had the white trim painted. When another realtor brought me an offer to purchase from her client she said that they thought the freshly painted trim looked very nice, but that there were two wires sticking out where the push button doorbell should be, and they supposed the painter had removed it and forgotten to put it back. I checked with the banker-seller and said we just couldn't find it and he answered, "Oh, we brought it with us. We thought we might want it."

Banker #3

I, after a traumatic divorce, was at last able to have my own quiet haven and was pleased with the unusual floor plan of my very own new home. I could hardly wait until settlement and made many trips to consider how I could put my own individual stamp on it. After all, my husband and I had built both of our homes and planned each detail, so taking an existing house and personalizing it was quite a challenge.

I knew the sellers and what they had in common with me, i.e., a divorce. The gentleman was a well-liked banker and his wife had taught my daughter in school. He was not taking the divorce well and was quite lonely, so he made several visits back to the house as I was busily painting furniture in the garage.

He started talking, hesitantly at first, and then, realizing that I was listening but not commenting, he plunged on: "Looking back, I think it all began at tennis. She started playing more and more and she came home with all these ideas. Do you know one night she said she wanted to go to Charlottesville to dinner? Not just that—at a Japanese restaurant!"

My heart immediately went out to Ruth, married to this man who admitted he was a "baseball nut" who had lunch at Rotary every single Tuesday and left for the bank and returned home at exactly the same time every day. Suddenly she wanted to tear down the fences around her schoolhouse regimen. He was lost!

Moving inside, I changed the subject to what he would agree to leave: the kitchen clock which was a plastic green stamp special but would go nicely with the sophisticated wallpaper I had selected. He agreed easily to that which made me happy.

Several days later, after settlement, I moved in with the help of my long-time maid. We wanted to get the kitchen settled first. I couldn't believe my eyes! The clock wasn't there! I asked Carrie, the maid, if she remembered a clock there.

"Yes, ma'am, I do," she said.

I said I wanted affirmation, so I would know I wasn't crazy. Reaching under the hanging cabinet for a paper towel I found no towel rack—another valuable attached article of plastic was missing!

Conclusions: 1. Bankers want to buy a bargain. 2. Bankers don't want to leave anything behind.

CHAPTER SIXTEEN

Hoarding

Although the term "hoarding" is understood by most people since it has been the subject of TV programs, 20 years ago most people were not really familiar with it unless, of course, they had encountered it with a family member or friend. In my 36 years of real estate service, I can only recall two instances of it, but they were completely unforgettable!

I had a client who was interested in a unique piece of property in Staunton—unique because it was in the downtown area and was a charming Victorian home situated on approximately one acre.

We stood on the gracious front porch after climbing many steps and I pushed open the heavy door. It was dark, so we stood still until our eyes adjusted to the sight—and what a sight! There were dusty volumes as well as old magazines no longer in print ascending the majestic stair case and antique velvet settees and wing chairs and floors surrounding us all piled high, almost as high as those tall ceilings with oil paintings, statuary, more books, and papers. I even spotted an "Old Nick" candy bar wrapper. (They hadn't been around for many, many years!) To move at all it had to be sideways and very gingerly. Most of the light was shut off by heavy velvet draperies with tattered brocade trim. I have no idea if the walls were painted or papered because we couldn't see them at all.

My only thought was, *This will never sell! If you can't see what you're getting, you'll never buy it.*

Just then I heard a tiny woman's voice from somewhere behind those floor-to-ceiling stacks of antique possessions saying, "It's just gotten beyond me!"

We tried to beat a hasty retreat but ended up saying polite things as we cautiously edged our way back out.

As it turned out two men with amazing vision bought the place, never having been able to see it well enough to know how much work lay ahead, and they turned it into an extremely lovely bed and breakfast as well as a popular restaurant. They turned the acreage into a large parking area, stone patios, and even a wedding chapel spot. As the years passed they purchased homes along the two sides of the long parking area and turned them into rental properties with very inviting antique-filled interiors! They also added onto the original Victorian home with a modern kitchen and a beautiful, light flooded room with many windows that allowed many people to dine there or hold events. These men did so much to improve and enhance that old section of our town and to attract tourism, a clean industry, to it! I remember that they offered free room and board to magazine writers who would go back to their towns and write about Staunton, Virginia.

The second hoarding story is more recent: It occurred in 1997. I had the fun of representing an entertaining person who was a very good friend of my daughter's. She had a great talent that was invaluable when it came to selling her small house: she was a born decorator and made the interior the most appealing that you could ever imagine! This offset the fact that it had only one bathroom! The hardest houses I ever had to sell had a single bathroom. I think it would still be on the market today if it hadn't been for her very inviting décor.

We started the house hunting process with lots of happy chatter because it was an exciting adventure to think of a bigger house (with two bathrooms!). She and her husband had a precious baby boy who needed a nice yard of some size for playing, so we started down the list.

We pulled in front of a nice traditional two-story home, reading the print out about it, and I shouted, "Look, Kathy! It has two full baths AND a large extra lot! Two level lots! How great!"

We couldn't wait to go in so I hurriedly tried the key in the front door lock and we attempted to enter. Together we exclaimed in one voice, "Look!"

It was absolutely crammed with boxes and boxes of stuff and we had to turn sideways to follow a narrow path through it! We wiggled to the left from what must have been the entrance hall into a room that seemed most like a living room with a couch covered with several blankets, a pillow, boxes with see-through cellophane lids housing large baby dolls, and many other boxes of various shapes and colors and kept staring in disbelief, especially when we saw a skeleton of a dead cat! There was a twisty, narrow path through this room with so many objects stacked so high on both sides! Eventually we forced our way into the kitchen, behind this room, and battled our way through brown paper bags and boxes to the sink.

I gasped. "Look, Kathy! A toothbrush and toothpaste beside the kitchen sink!" It dawned on us at the same instant that the owner must sleep on the couch and brush her teeth in the kitchen. But why?

Next, we slowly progressed up the steps, littered with toys, boxes, bags, and some magazines. The master bedroom lay ahead with a bed over on the right that was piled so high we knew no one could possibly sleep there. Wrestling with the closet door we saw baby clothes still with tags on them—never worn—in their original boxes and more toys, girl dolls, boy dolls, of all shapes and sizes.

I asked, "Do you think we should find the bathroom?"

I put my shoulder to the door and, after several tries, forced it open. We could barely make out where the fixtures lay hidden under garbage bags crammed with dolls and doll clothes! I reached over to the sink and tried a faucet, but no water came out. Then it dawned on Kathy that the owner must take sponge baths at the kitchen sink!

We slowly navigated our path down the staircase, out the kitchen door, and into the yard. Aha! The big, level, double lot that lay in back under gigantic shade trees!

Turning to me Kathy asked, "When can we come back? I want Tom to see it!"

I was slightly incredulous! "You do? Really?" I asked.

The brave young couple decided that the yard was already perfect for them and that the house could be too! They went home and started enlisting their good friends to help them clean, tear off old wallpaper, and pull up carpet after closing!

The days clicked by quickly and we went to the property the day before settlement to do a "walk through" and make sure it was cleaned out and ready for them to occupy. What did we see? All the furniture, boxes, EVERYTHING of hers was still there.

Panicked, we called the listing realtor who said, "Oh, it will be cleared by closing."

We answered that we didn't see how!

That evening we went by again and there was a huge moving van in front. We said that we didn't see how it would be ready for possession after the closing at l0:00 am the next day to which the big, burly moving man replied that he had orders to work all night and get it completely cleaned out.

We definitely had our doubts but found out later that he had transported all of it, every last box, to eight storage units, and that the owner had moved into an apartment.

It is a showplace today and soon a wedding will take

place in that beautiful backyard which will also be adorned with a large tent for the guests.

Summing up my two experiences with HOARDER HOUSE BUYERS, I would say that their vision served them very well and actually saved these properties from falling into ruin.

Motto: There are two ways to destroy property: 1. Bomb it. 2. Neglect it. Both have the same effect.

CHAPTER SEVENTEEN

Once there was a young couple with two children who wanted to move to Staunton, so they drove around looking for a neighborhood they liked with a nice building lot. They were delighted to find one with a spectacular tree in front. They wrote an offer at once and after it was accepted, they made several trips to the lot with house plans in hand.

One day, they drove up to the lot and yelled "Where's the tree?" It had been levelled to the ground! They were so upset and so glad they were able to withdraw their offer. They decided that they really liked the neighborhood, so they decided to look at the house I had for sale there. I had on high heels, tripped on a loose carpet edge at the top of the stairs, and fell into the client's arms. We still laugh about me "falling for him," as he said!

He and his wife decided to buy the house, although it wasn't the ideal floor plan they would have built!

Meanwhile, the lot's owner was very upset about losing his buyers, so he made it a point to find out who had cut the tree down. He discovered that it was someone else's builder who had followed his orders and chopped down a tree—the only trouble was that the lot where he was to do this was about nine lots away! As punishment, he had to buy the treeless lot and pay full price for it!

SECTION FIVE
HOME LAYOUTS

CHAPTER EIGHTEEN

Floor Plans

When I started my real estate career in 1977, all "rec" rooms were in the basement. The main floor usually had a small entrance hall, large living room, dining room, and a small den with fireplace. Bedrooms in a two-story were always upstairs. Bathrooms were fairly small and utilitarian rather than luxurious and many times there were 1½ baths, and in larger traditional floor plans 2½ baths were normal.

When the 1980's dawned, I spoke to several clients who yearned for a house with a big family room off the kitchen. No one wanted a small, cozy den. I believe that TV had a lot to do with it. TV shows became popular entertainment and you needed a bigger informal room for everyone to sit in—the whole family—hence a "family room." Mothers wanted it off the kitchen, so they could supervise young children who were playing or watching TV in that room.

It wasn't too long after that that we heard the term "great room." People moving here from western states were used to this floor plan in which the kitchen and family room were combined, and you could dine in them. I remember when people started demanding them and we went into a full-blown panic because our little traditional southern town didn't have even one house with that open floor plan. I remember one particular client who loved that plan and could easily buy one, but the nearest one at that time was about 27 miles north of here, so no sale!

Mistakes Builders Have Made

I saw many small homes go up quickly and sell well when the market was good and I saw many builders get fat and happy. They decided to build bigger, more expensive homes and do even better.

When I entered one of these I realized what was wrong, right away! They were building the same general non-luxurious floor plan but with larger rooms. I told them that in this higher price range the buyer had different demands and a different life style. He wanted a formal dining room and not a small breakfast room sized dining area for example. There are many differences in lifestyle that the builders simply didn't realize.

I represented another builder who took an attractive house plan and put it on a high lot with a drop-dead view of The Blue Ridge Mountains. The trouble was that the big windows were in the back of the house with a view of the steep cliff behind the house and in front the windows were quite small! That was slow S-L-O-W to sell!

The quality of new "spec" homes in our area took a dive in the 60's when cheaper materials were used. Corners were cut in many places and I shuddered when a buyer would say to me, "I don't need a home inspection on a new house."

I would say, "You especially need one on a new house."

Much to my horror, I saw staples used instead of nails and fiberboard inside of closets where wood used to be!

There was a short period of time when "spec" houses were about the same floor plan: three bedrooms, two bath ranch, no basement, and eat-in kitchen. The walls were white and there was wall-to-wall carpet (often gray) everywhere except baths and kitchen. When you opened the door your eyes watered from the chemicals released from this house that was shut up tight and couldn't breathe at all! Fortunately, this period was short-lived.

It has been interesting to see the once formal entertaining rooms disappear into one huge "great room." I note with a touch of nostalgia the disappearance of the very large dining room so necessary in the Victorian Era because meal time was so important in bringing the family together at one time and I think we've lost something of great value there.

Some old American towns such as Staunton (founded in the 1700's) had Victorian homes as well as Colonial homes from The Federal Period and even authentic, original log cabins, and I've sold them all. We have many charming Victorians with a baby's room in front, often adjoining two large, high ceiling front bedrooms. I watched that room become a sewing room for a few years and then suddenly no one sewed anymore so it was turned into a small office or a walk-in closet.

Speaking of closets, in the days of Jefferson and Madison and other illustrious Virginia presidents, each room was taxed so there were no closets—only wardrobes—because closets were considered small rooms. It's interesting what you learn in real estate!

Now in the 2010-2018 years homes have changed floor plans again! A two-story home sells better with the master suite on the main floor, and if you really want to do it up right, there's another possible master suite on the second floor. Both lead to luxurious spa-like bathrooms, as big as a bedroom, with jetted tub outfitted with candles, huge showers with many showerheads and a seat, his and her sinks, and dressing areas. A huge family room is on the main floor and a half bath for guests. The kitchen has beautiful cabinetry and should, since it's on display from the porch or deck, family room, and formal areas.

There are even "McMansions" built now with an amazing number of square feet, work out rooms, indoor and outdoor pools, tennis courts, home theaters, and anything else the heart desires!

SECTION SIX
THE NUTS AND BOLTS OF BUYING AND SELLING

CHAPTER NINETEEN

Where Do I Start When Buying a House?

Let me begin by saying where NOT to start! I've had phone calls from people "driving around" who see a real estate sign and call the listing office to inquire how much that house is. Ninety-five percent of the time these people are clueless because they have no ideas what they can afford so it's just a waste of time to throw a number to them. THEY ARE STARTING AT THE WRONG PLACE!

What is the right place? Well, a prospective buyer needs to actually make time for about a 30-minute appointment at their bank or a mortgage company and not to just get prequalified for a certain loan amount but preapproved. With a letter of preapproval, they have ammunition to present to the Seller which is valuable any time but absolutely invaluable when their offer is in competition!

Prequalified can be defined as, "According to what

you've told me, you should qualify for the loan amount you're asking for." But if you're preapproved, the lender has run tests on your income and has your entire financial picture and therefore can issue a preapproval letter.

Your lender can keep your information on file and quickly pull it out when you've made a buying decision.

CHAPTER TWENTY

PREPARE FOR SELLING WELL IN ADVANCE

I knew that the day would come when my parents would need to sell their home and go to a retirement community, so I decided to start searching for the ideal realtor in advance.

I lived several states away, so I took my real estate credentials with me when I visited with them. I went to the Indianapolis Board of Realtors and was allowed to seat myself in their spacious building and look up realtors.

After about seventeen years in the business at that point, I knew exactly what qualities in a realtor I was seeking, and I preselected one! There was just one out of thousands. I wanted someone with the right professional degrees, the right number of years in the business, and who really knew how desirable that location was in a city so huge—someone from that neighborhood.

I was lucky to find anyone who met my rigorous standards and was I right! She examined the professional appraisal and confided in me that due to the demand for that peaceful little street with its beautiful trees, and its proximity to one of the major streets, the asking price could run $10,000 to $15,000 more than the appraisal! She felt it in her bones because she grew up there!

CHAPTER TWENTY-ONE

MORE MISTAKES TO AVOID, WHETHER YOU'RE A BUYER OR A SELLER

There is absolutely nothing more local than the real estate market, so how can someone in a cozy office who works for a company like "Willow" or "SuperRealtor. com" (names changed to protect the guilty) possibly know that there's a high demand for charming homes all along Sunrise Street, but on the street parallel to it there is practically no demand at all? For the same number of square feet, a house on Sunrise could bring a much higher price!

SuperRealtor.com tries to cover the entire housing market as well! It's known for inaccuracies such as stating that a home was built in 1911 when in reality the home is 11 years old! This happened to me and my sellers wanted this corrected at once, but I was unable to get it corrected with this huge company.

Buyers make mistakes too, such as expecting a home to be as utterly perfect as a TV show shows homes to be. Homes people actually live in are not as neat and perfect as homes on a TV set!

CHAPTER TWENTY-TWO

REGARDING BUYERS

Typically, many realtors go through their entire career not getting it. I have heard so many say, "All buyers are liars." This simply isn't the case at all. All realtors need to listen to what buyers say they are looking for and then they need to keep asking questions. They need to understand the buyer's motivation. Is this a job promotion? Is this a downsize move for some reason? Is this buyer buying safety for his children in a dead-end street situation?

You see, buyers will ALWAYS compromise specification, but they will NEVER compromise motivation. To illustrate:

A buyer moving here from out of state who is an officer in a large corporation says, "I must have a living room that's at least 15' X 20'."

Your average Realtor will go through listing after listing trying to find those measurements that's specified.

What's the motivation? Well, he's been given a new position and a raise, so he wants to have an impressive home to entertain members of his company. You find a house with a living room that's 15' X 18' – not quite the specification the buyer wants.

You sell the house you hope he'll buy like this:

Drive down the street saying, "Hi, Dr. Smith." You can add, "He's such a nice fellow." Drive further and, if you don't see the people, explain who the neighbors are (i.e., "That's Judge Brown's house."). By the time you reach the driveway, you have it sold.

CHAPTER
TWENTY-THREE

WRONG! WRONG! WRONG!

Among the many mistakes people make about real estate is the notion that the longer a potential Buyer spends looking at a house, the more interested he is.

Many times, a Buyer is on a strict schedule, so he has in hand a list of perhaps 10 houses that he wants to see in the one day he has. He goes through them, maybe taking notes, and selects one, or a few to go back and revisit as soon as his schedule permits because they hold some interest for him.

Then, of course, there's the impulse Buyer!

I once had a lovely ranch home listed on several acres with a nice barn and a little stream. I chatted in the garage with the seller while the prospective buyer and her realtor went through the large brick ranch. You couldn't have counted to 10 before they emerged and thanked us! I asked the other realtor if they had seen the basement door and the prospective buyer answered, "Oh, I don't do basements--don't like them."

The seller commented as they drove away, "Well, that wasn't much of a showing!" Do you know that a few hours later I was meeting with that seller with a full price offer in hand from that lady who was no longer a "prospective" buyer, but the "real buyer"!

Appraisals

I thought a word about appraisals would be in order at this time. Let me tell you how they come in to play in a real estate transaction just from my 36 years of experience.

Of course, as we all know, banks use appraisals as a step in making the loan to a qualified buyer. I once had a TV program on WVIRTV, NBC, Charlottesville, the purpose of which was to help the public understand the rather complicated process of buying and selling real estate. One of my three guests was an appraiser who has been in the business some 40 odd years and had his own appraisal company. In interviewing him, I asked how long a bank honors a professional appraisal and he said it was honored for three months.

In surprise, I said, "Just for three months?"

He replied, "Yes, as you know the economy can be impacted by a number of factors, such as factories opening to factories closing, interest rates going up or down, and such."

We then discussed how important it was to have a date right near the signature on a professional appraisal and of course each appraisal states that "as of this date my opinion of the value is…."

You can see from this discussion that property doesn't automatically appreciate just because it is now a later date than the appraisal that had been made. Sometimes it stays the same or actually depreciates.

The next point I would like to make is that an appraisal is, by definition, an opinion of value. Knowing this, a large company in our area used to automatically order two appraisals (by two different professional appraisers) each time one of their employees needed to sell and relocate. The CEO told me years ago that if the appraisals were more than 5% apart they would then order a third appraisal.

The appraiser's choice of which three comparable properties has a great influence on the resulting appraised value of the property and with this knowledge the appraiser tries to obtain comparable properties as near to the subject property geographically as possible and as similar in the important respects—that is to say the respects that are important to him as an appraiser—as possible.

Appraisers consider the importance and indeed the measurable features to include the above criteria and square footage, acreage, etc. While these factors are not to be ignored I would like to stress here that many other features are important to the homebuyer which are impossible to measure. These include the floor plan and its flow, the updates—particularly in the kitchen and bathrooms—the decorating, whether there are hardwood floors, the square footage of the master bedroom and how their furniture will fit, the square footage of the master bath and how luxurious it might be, the size of the closets, etc. Since women make more home buying decisions than men, you can understand how important these niceties are to her. Accordingly, in each price range we find that the buyers' level of expectations differs as to these last-mentioned features.

Appraisal is an "art," not a "science." This is unfortunate but true and is illustrated by the fact that appraisers may choose different comparables to use in determining which are most appropriate to measure the worth of the subject property. His own personal likes and dislikes will figure subconsciously into his thinking because he is not a robot but rather a human being. For example, if he hates Victorian architecture he probably will not value it as highly as someone who loves it. This is just a part of being human.

Another fact may interest you. Appraisers have often called me to ask my opinion about their conclusion and the comparables they are using, particularly with higher priced properties. They know I do a lot of work in this area and that I have been inside those kitchens and bathrooms and floor plans and they are aware of how important these things are when they are choosing comparables to a subject property which they have been in but of course they have not seen the other properties inside. I feel that is a great responsibility and I do the best I can to be helpful to them.

In light of all of these statements, I feel that an appraisal, or an opinion of value, as of a certain date, is one of the tools that is of some value in selling the property. I do not feel that it is the "be all" and "end all" and it is not the whole story. It is a spring board from which to negotiate, in my opinion. Further, I feel it is the most effective in garnering a price close to what a good appraisal predicts in the beginning of the listing period when the property is new and exciting on the market. As time goes on it becomes "shop worn" because of the length of time it's been on the market. Market time is extremely important in realizing a price which is near a professional appraisal. A comparison might be drawn by using the phrase "God's time" as compared to the sellers' personal time table. These can be very different time tables.

FINAL CHAPTER AND FINAL WORDS

I know of nothing that reveals a person's true character more than a real estate transaction.

I have seen a seller carefully arrange logs in the fireplace of a log cabin for the buyer's first fire and I've seen sellers take their doorbell and mailbox with them.

I've seen a seller brag that he would get his price and then pay a lot of a purchaser's closing costs in order to have his asking price show up in print as the selling price.

I've seen loud arguments at the closing table and watched in fascination to see who would prevail.

One closing I remember well occurred many years ago after the purchasers did a "walk through" of the county farmhouse before settlement. They came storming into their attorney's office ranting because the generator in the garage didn't work. The seller said that it hadn't worked for years, but that it was big and heavy so they just left it in the garage. The buyer cried that it was a system and that all systems were supposed to be in working order at closing. The attorney put in a call to the sellers' attorney and soon she appeared and soon she appeared, arguing as she came through the door and slid into her seat. She said that piece of equipment was NOT a system. And so it went until it escalated into a shouting match between the lawyers! At last it was decided that it was indeed not a system.

Another exciting closing I remember came about because the buyer started raving that the house that the house had termites so he wouldn't buy it. The termite report stated that it didn't have them. The closing attorney left the office and together with the buyer they drove to the house. The living room floor swayed a little in one spot so they pulled up carpeting and there, between some boards, were some happy little termites chewing away! Of course, the repairs had to be made!

I never had a dull day as a realtor because I never had the same day twice.

www.ingramcontent.com/pod-product-compliance
Lightning Source LLC
Chambersburg PA
CBHW022338280326
41934CB00006B/682